EGYPTOLOGY

THE COLORING BOOK

Based on the
Journal of

Miss
Emily Sands

November 1926 —

CANDLEWICK PRESS

PUBLISHERS OF RARE & UNUSUAL BOOKS

Arrival at Cairo

Monday 1st November 1926

Yesterday I had my first glimpse of the pyramids on the train to Cairo. Potent symbols of the mysterious land of Egypt, they reminded me of all I have come to discover—the dusty tombs, the ornate temples, the golden treasures, and the strange, unearthly mummies.

I arranged to meet my fellow Egypt enthusiasts, the writers and artists who are to help compile my journal, in the foyer of Patsy's Hotel in Cairo. There, I spoke to some archaeologists who are going out to Giza. They told me that excavations in Egypt—near the pyramids and elsewhere—continue apace, with exciting discoveries being made on an almost daily basis!

N.H. set out early to sketch these archaeologists surveying the Giza plateau.

The Farncombe Papyrus

Monday 1st November 1926

In the wake of the magnificent discoveries recently made here in Egypt by Howard Carter, I, like so many others, was struck with a sudden passion for all things Egyptological. Being a friend of the Farncombe family, I had heard of their old papyrus (right), and I asked Lady Amanda Farncombe if I could take a look at it. As I examined it, she told me how one well-known Egyptologist had suggested it might just hold a clue to the lost tomb of Osiris. That same day the subject of an expedition was raised, which Amanda generously offered to fund herself. She and her husband have even come to Cairo to bid us farewell and "bon voyage!"

Right, H.W.'s drawing of the Farncombe Papyrus. The two lines of hieroglyphs on the left side of the papyrus read: "Isis, Lady of Heaven, Mistress of the Gods, She grants that you may live for ever and eternity." On the right: "Osiris, the great god, foremost in the West, Lord of Busiris, who is in the Holy Mound."

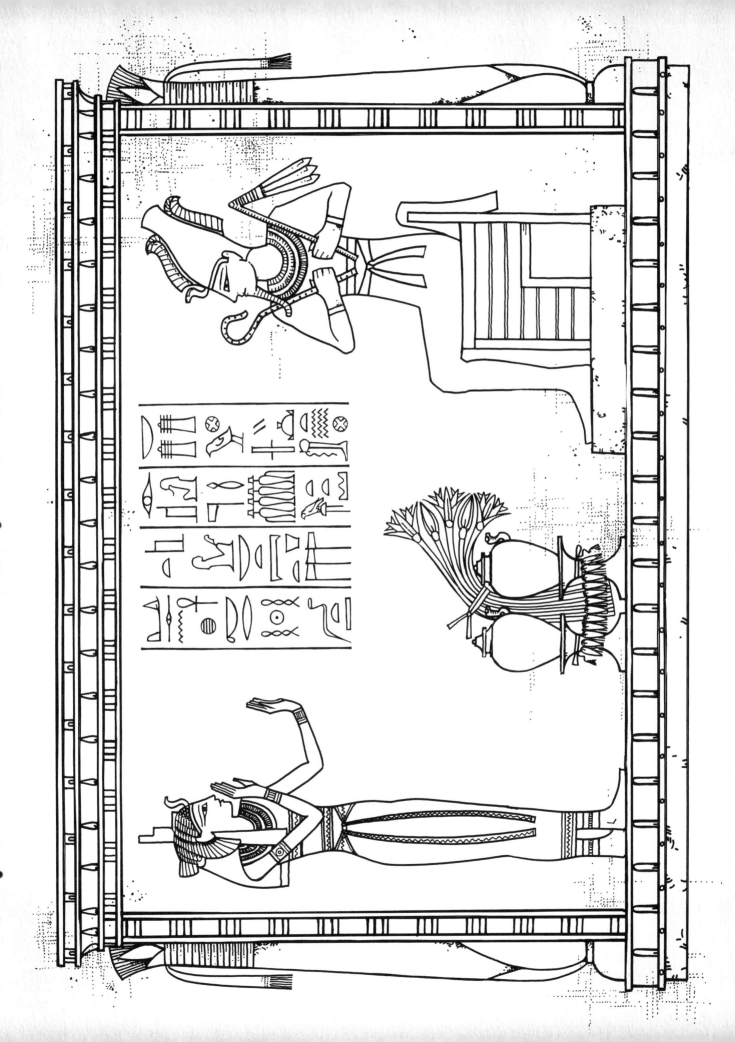

Cairo Museum

Monday 1st November 1926

As Cairo has the very best collection of Egyptian antiquities anywhere in the world, I went to the museum to learn about the history of Ancient Egypt. Although I have hired the services of Mr. Taak, a much-travelled interpreter, or "dragoman," the museum curators spoke either French or English and were very helpful.

At the museum I asked one curator if he had heard the story of a "lost tomb of Osiris" hidden in a "holy mound." He laughed and said it all sounded like nonsense, but when I showed him the papyrus, he asked us where exactly we had got it, as it looked so authentic!

At the museum, H.W. painted the statues of Rahotep and Nofret. H.W. also drew this bracelet of Queen Ahotep and a wooden statue of King Awibre Hor.

*Bracelet of
Queen Ahotep*

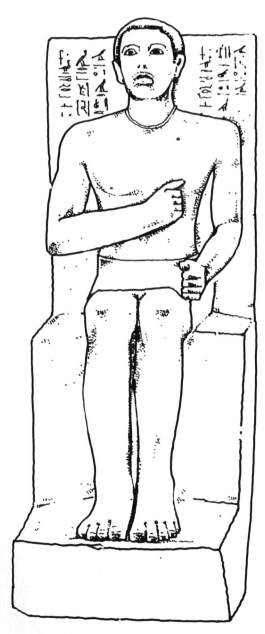

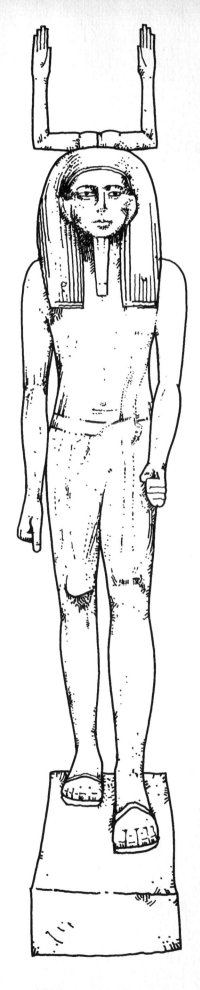

Rahotep

Nofret

King Awibre Hor

Sailing the Nile

Monday 1st November 1926

In order to travel up the River Nile, I have hired an old-fashioned dahabeeyah, or sailing barge. It comes complete with its own captain and crew and is called the "Bennu Bird." The prevailing wind on the Nile blows from the north, so our boat will easily be able to sail upstream as we journey south. Our return journey will be made using the river current to carry us along, and will be considerably slower, allowing us ample time to reflect on the many wonders we will have seen—and to revisit our favourite spots.

Bennu Bird

Notes on Ancient Egypt

Monday 8th November 1926

Despite the curator's doubts, I am not going to give up my search for the lost tomb just yet. Instead I have decided to make a few notes about some of the Egyptian gods. There were hundreds of Ancient Egyptian gods, but the ones I am interested in are those linked to Osiris.

ISIS Wife of Osiris, Isis found the scattered parts of her husband's body. She used them to make the first mummy, which she buried in secret and protected with powerful spells.

OSIRIS Legend tells that Osiris, murdered king of Upper and Lower Egypt, ruled for a great many years before becoming lord of the underworld after his death. Could this story be a memory of a real king?

HORUS Son and avenger of Osiris, hawk-headed Horus became king of Egypt after his father's death. He ruled justly, and many temples were raised in his worship.

SETH The enemy of Osiris, his brother Seth coveted the throne of Egypt. It is said that, after he killed Osiris, Seth cut the body into pieces and hid them in fourteen secret locations.

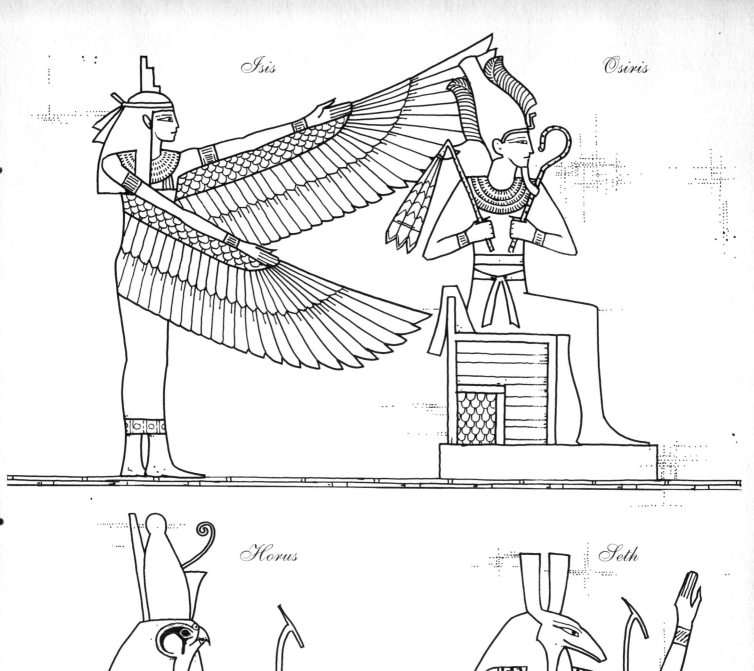

Isis

Osiris

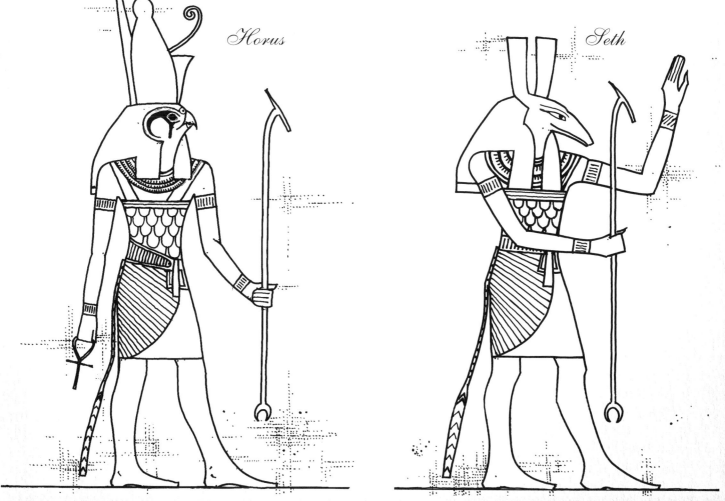

Horus

Seth

A Trip to Giza

Tuesday 9th November 1926

Before setting off on our river journey, we took the tram out to the Giza plateau to visit the pyramids. Mr. Taak, our guide, provided camels for us to ride and suggested that a confident approach to mounting the beasts would be best, leapfrogging into the saddle from behind. My camel did not take too kindly to this and set off at a vigorous pace before finally settling down. When it comes to the independent traveller riding camels, it is often the camels who decide just how "independent" each ride is going to be!

As we climbed about with torches inside the tunnels and chambers of the pyramids—a welcome respite from our dromedary transports—Mr. Taak told us how these monuments were built originally as the tombs of some of the Old Kingdom pharaohs.

The Great Sphinx

Tuesday 9th November 1926

The oldest known monumental sculpture in the world, the Great Sphinx of Giza is a limestone statue cut from the bedrock. Its face is that of King Khaefra and it looks directly east, ready to greet the rising sun.

We were lucky indeed to find the Sphinx cleared of sand for the first time in 2,000 years! For most of its life, it was buried up to its neck. It seems that even during ancient times it used to get covered in sand. Tuthmosis IV, who lived a thousand years after the statue was built, told a story about how he fell asleep near the Sphinx and the statue came to him in a dream and told him that it would make him pharaoh in return for digging it out!

It is amazing to think that the Ancient Egyptians could build such wonderful monuments using no more than simple tools of copper and stone.

Saqqara and Memphis

Friday 12th November 1926

It has only taken a couple of days to sail the "Bennu Bird" from Cairo to Badrashein, where we travelled by donkey to Saqqara, the burial ground of Memphis, Egypt's most ancient capital. We plan to see the Step Pyramid of Zoser, the Serapeum—catacomb of the sacred Apis bulls—and a remarkable tomb of animal and bird mummies.

Following a clue left by the Greek geographer Strabo, Auguste Mariette located the Serapeum in 1851. There the Apis bulls—considered incarnations of the god Ptah—were buried in huge sarcophagi that weigh up to eighty tons. At Saqqara, the Apis bulls were mummified with a care usually reserved only for the pharaoh himself. Right, N.H. has reimagined this scene wonderfully.

The Tomb of the Bird Mummies

Friday 12th November 1926

At the Tomb of the Bird Mummies lie the remains of perhaps millions of ibises and baboons (sacred to the god Thoth) and cats (sacred to Bast), along with snakes, crocodiles, frogs, and many other creatures. It is sad to think that these creatures were bred and sold to be sacrificed to the gods, although not all of the wrappings contain animal remains. Some Ancient Egyptians who thought they were buying an ibis or a cat were being fooled into buying a fake packet of rags!

Although we could not gain access to this tomb as it is considered too dangerous, the guards were happy to show us a few examples—which H.W. quickly made drawings of—and even offered to sell us one of the fakes. Of course, I declined. After all, how am I to know if I am buying a genuine fake?

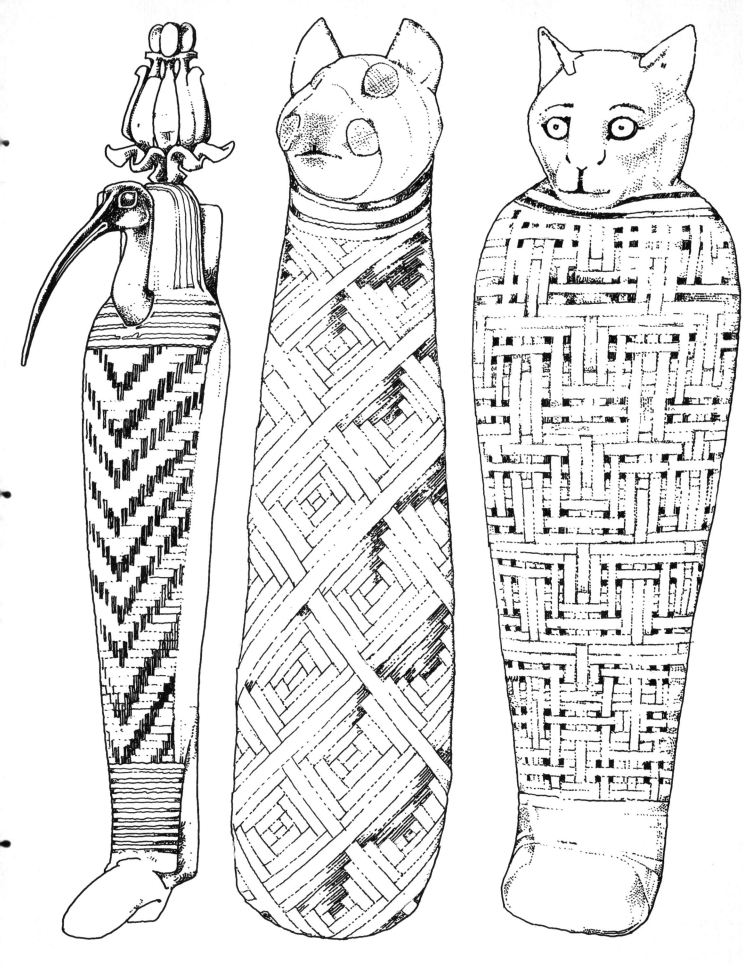

Mummified ibis   *Mummified cats*

King Zoser's Pyramid

Friday 12th November 1926

We arrived at the site of the Step Pyramid of King Zoser in the middle of a sandstorm of such ferocity that I wondered, for a moment, if the Egyptian gods were expressing their anger at our expedition. Mr. Taak, however, reassured us that sandstorms, while infrequent, usually last an hour or two at most. We therefore retreated to the "Bennu Bird" to wait out the storm.

While we did, Mr. Taak explained that pharaohs before Zoser were usually buried in mastaba tombs of mud brick. Zoser went one better, commissioning his royal architect Imhotep to build a step pyramid of stone, surrounded by walls that represented the walls of Memphis itself. In the Step Pyramid, a statue of King Zoser was found completely walled up, except for a slit at eye level so the king could gaze out on eternity. Could there be a statue like this in the tomb of Osiris?

Tel el Amana, Queen Nefertiti

Saturday 27th November 1926

The wind having dropped, we discovered that the motor on our dahabeeyah was out of action, and so it had to be hauled up the last stretch of river to reach the tombs of Beni Hasan.

South of Beni Hasan we visited the ruins at Tel el Amarna. This city, known as Akhetaten, was built by the heretic Pharaoh Akhenaten to be Egypt's new capital. He banned the worship of Egypt's old gods in favour of a single god, the Aten. After Pharaoh Akhenaten's death, the city was razed to the ground by his successors, and his name was chiselled out of history.

This bust of Nefertiti, Akhenaten's queen, was found in the ruins of a sculptor's studio at Akhetaten in 1911, sketched by H.W.

Pharaoh Akhenaten

Saturday 27th November 1926

This sketch by H.W. shows a relief of Akhenaten and his family worshipping the Aten—represented by the rays of the sun. At the top is a series of hieroglyphs.

The secret of understanding hieroglyphs was lost until Jean Francois Champollion interpreted the writing on a stone found near Rosetta in 1799. The famous Rosetta Stone at long last enabled Champollion to decipher hieroglyphs, as the Egyptian scribes had written on it in three scripts (hieroglyphics, demotic Egyptian, and Greek). By comparing the texts, Champollion was able to recognize the names of Ptolemy and Cleopatra.

At Sacred Abydos

Friday 10th December 1926

At last we have arrived at Abydos, the most sacred site in all Egypt, and the centre of Osiris worship. Here, behind the temple of Seti I, father of Rameses II, there is a mysterious, half-flooded temple known as the Osireion. I have made contact here with a friend of Lady Farncombe—an archaeologist called Gordon John—and he has promised to give us a proper tour of the whole site.

Mr. John took us to see the tomb of King Djer. He told us that in Middle Kingdom times it was thought to have been the tomb of Osiris. I showed Mr. John our papyrus, and he said that while Abydos could be ruled out as the site of the "holy mound," a site near Philae might just be a contender.

N.H. drew this re-creation of the scene of the daily dressing of the god Horus in the temple. Each day his statue was dressed by the priests, and fresh offerings were placed before him as hymns of praise were sung out.

Deir El Bahri

Sunday 12th December 1926

We have been on board the "Bennu Bird" for just over a month now. To pass the time, we often play a game called Senet, a sort of Ancient Egyptian checkers. But we will not have much time for play today, because we are going to visit Deir El Bahri, the sacred mortuary temple of Queen Hatshepsut.

Near the ruins of the tomb-builders' village of Deir El Medina, we had an eerie moonlight encounter with a jackal by one of the old tombs. I could almost fancy it was the jackal-god Anubis himself watching us.

Soon we will enter the Valley of the Kings. I very much hope to meet Howard Carter, to see whether he has any useful ideas about our lost tomb.

Egyptian Voyages

Sunday 12th December 1926

Mr. Taak informed us that the Ancient Egyptians appeared to have had no desire to travel to foreign parts. They firmly believed Egypt to be the best of all possible lands. However, they did conduct trading expeditions in order to bring back goods such as leopard skins for their priests, as well as spices, incense, and wood. The palm trees that grew in Egypt were useless for construction, so cedar was imported from Byblos, in Lebanon.

H.W. copied these pictures of one expedition to Punt, an African land that may have lain along the shore of the Red Sea. In the top picture, we can see the King and Queen of Punt coming to greet the Egyptians. In the middle, we can see the stilt houses of the people of Punt, and in the lower one, Egyptians carrying incense trees back to their ships in wicker baskets, to be watered regularly on the trip home.

The Valley of the Kings
Thursday 16th December 1926

Arriving in the valley, I had very much hoped to meet
Howard Carter, but he was indisposed. I suppose this may
just have something to do with the fact that the tomb
he uncovered—of Tutankhamen—has had some 20,000
visitors since he first opened it up in 1922.

When Carter opened the tomb, he first made a small hole
in the tomb door and looked in. After waiting for some
time, Carter's expedition companion Lord Carnarvon grew
impatient.
"Can you see anything?" he asked.
"Yes," replied Carter. "Wonderful things!"

Right: the priceless mask of the pharaoh, made from
22 1/2 pounds of solid gold and found on the mummy
itself.

The Famous Tomb

Thursday 16th December 1926

Carter has so far cleared the antechamber and burial
chamber, the result of four years' painstaking work.
Currently he is unwrapping Tutankhamen's mummy. Made
of gold foil on carved wood, the outer coffin is the
first in a series of coffins that fit like Russian dolls
over the mummy resting inside. The second coffin is
much like the outer coffin, but slightly smaller, and
reproduces the pharaoh's features. The third coffin is
made of about 240 pounds of solid gold. It's the single
largest piece of ancient gold workmanship ever to have
been discovered anywhere in the world.

Howard Carter has found a whole host of charms, amulets,
and jewels among the mummy wrappings. These items were
designed to protect the king in the afterlife.

The mummy itself shall be returned to his tomb after
Carter's autopsy as a mark of respect for both Pharaoh
Tutankhamen's status and great antiquity.

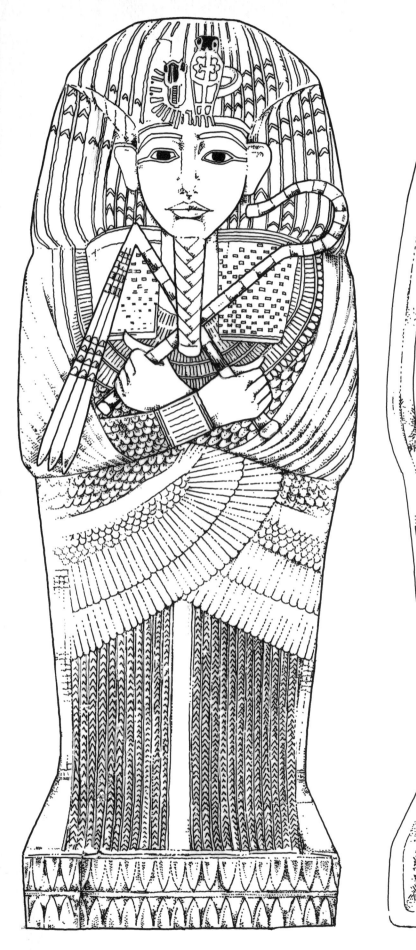

Outer coffin

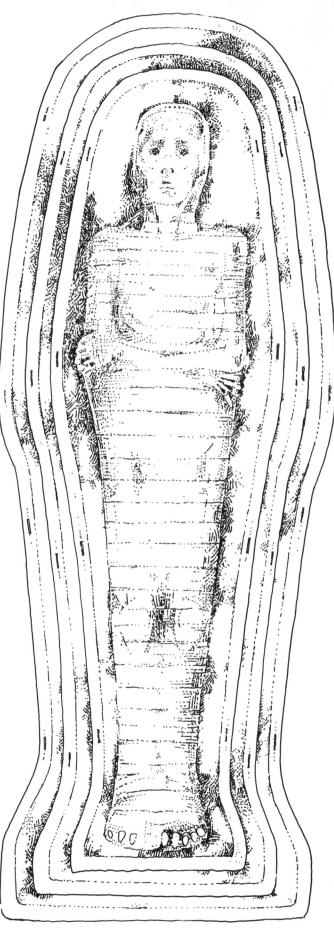

Inner coffins and mummy

Canopic Jars

Thursday 16th December 1926

When a person was mummified, their internal organs were placed in canopic jars guarded by different gods. So far, Carter has not found the chest containing the canopic jars in King Tutankhamen's tomb. They will probably look like these:

FALCON JAR The falcon-headed god Qebehsenuef was protector of the intestines.

HUMAN JAR The liver was placed in the god Imsety's jar. He had a human head.

JACKAL JAR The jackal-headed god Duamutef guarded the stomach of the deceased in his jar.

BABOON JAR The lungs were stored in the jar of the baboon-headed god Hapi.

Falcon jar

Human jar

Jackal jar

Baboon jar

The King's Burial Chamber

Thursday 16th December 1926

Although his tomb contains some of the most wonderful and precious antiquities ever found, we were told that King Tutankhamen himself was not a very powerful monarch and that his short reign ended when he was only about nineteen years old. How magnificent, then, must have been the lost funerary treasures of some of Egypt's mightiest pharaohs, such as Khufu (Cheops), Khaefra (Chephren), or Rameses II!

Right: a painting from the wall of the king's burial chamber by H.W.

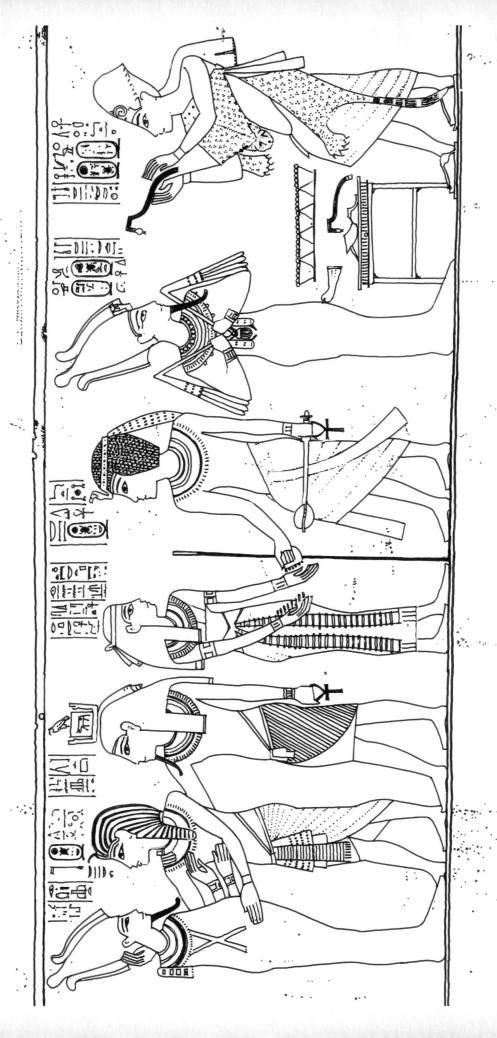

The Singing Statues of Memnon

Saturday 18th December 1926

As we approached Luxor, site of the Ancient Egyptian capital of Thebes, we were caught in another fierce sandstorm as we followed the famous avenue of sphinxes from the Temple of Karnak to the Temple of Luxor. Across the river we visited the famous "singing statues" of Memnon—two huge sandstone colossi that stand some 60 feet high.

These colossi, which used to be known as "Shammy" and "Tammy," possibly a corruption of the Arabic words for left and right, used to "sing" each morning—a sound probably caused as the sun heated up the stones. But the singing stopped when Roman emperor Septimus Severus "repaired" them in AD 199.

The southern statue (left-hand side of picture) shows Pharaoh Amenhotep III with his wife, Tiy, and a daughter. The northern statue (right-hand side of picture) shows the pharaoh with his mother, Mutemwia.

The Theban Triad

Saturday 18th December 1926

Near the site of ancient Thebes, the Temple of Karnak looks glorious from the river. There are 134 columns in the Great Hypostyle Hall in the temple itself, one of the most photographed and impressive sites in all of Egypt.

At Karnak we learned that most Ancient Egyptian cities had their own triads of gods, a triad being a father, mother, and son. Here, Amun, Mut, and their son, Khonsu, were worshipped. Khonsu was represented as a gigantic Egyptian baby, with a child's shaved head and sidelock of hair.

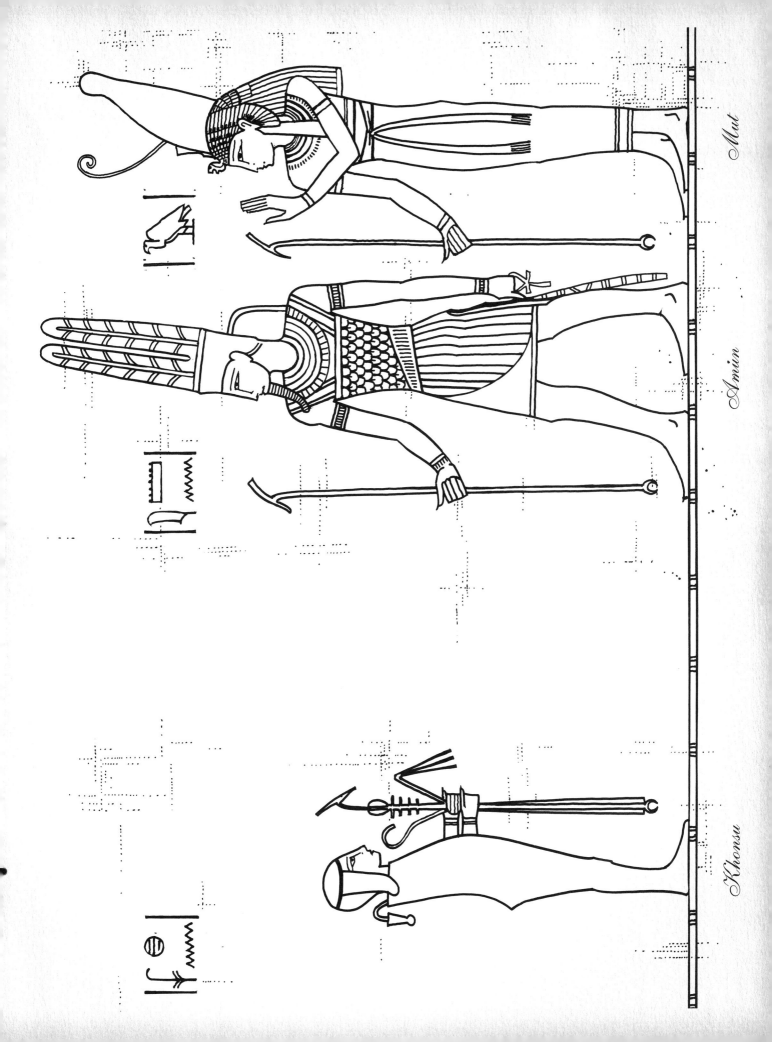

Mut

Amun

Khonsu

A Postcard from Luxor

Saturday 18th December 1926

At Luxor I bought this amusing postcard that shows two huge feet from the Ramesseum—the inspiration for a famous poem by Shelley.

OZYMANDIAS

I met a traveller from an antique land
Who said: Two vast and trunkless legs of stone
Stand in the desert. Near them, on the sand,
Half sunk, a shattered visage lies, whose frown,
And wrinkled lip, and sneer of cold command,
Tell that its sculptor well those passions read
Which yet survive, stamped on these lifeless things,
The hand that mocked them, and the heart that fed,
And on the pedestal these words appear:
"My name is Ozymandias, king of kings:
Look on my works, ye Mighty, and despair!"
Nothing beside remains. Round the decay
Of that colossal wreck, boundless and bare,
The lone and level sands stretch far away.
—Percy Bysshe Shelley (1792–1822)

Whilst in Luxor, Mr. Taak introduced us to a young Egyptian man who claimed to know all about the tomb of Osiris. He entrusted to us a strange Eye of Re amulet. Before we leave town, I am going to commission a goldsmith to make me a copy of it to take back to Lady Farncombe.

The City of the Hawk

Saturday 25th December 1926

It is Christmas Day! And so we are celebrating in style with a pudding that H.W. has brought all the way from London! It is just what I need to cheer me up as, despite my mysterious encounter at Luxor, I don't seem to be getting any closer to Osiris or his tomb.

In the morning we visited the ruins of Hieraconpolis, city of the hawk. Hieraconpolis was the home of Upper Egypt's early kings. Here, we learned that the followers of Horus of Hieraconpolis defeated the followers of Seth of Nubt in battle. Could this have anything to do with the origins of the Osiris legend?

Right: This gold hawk head, with eyes of obsidian, was found nearby (N.H.).

The Narmer Palette

Saturday 25th December 1926

At an incredible 5,000 years old, the Narmer Palette—found in the Temple of Horus—contains some of the earliest hieroglyphic inscriptions ever found and is in almost perfect condition. It shows the pharaoh Narmer, wearing the white crown of Upper Egypt, defeating a rival king and unifying the Nile kingdoms. On the other side, the pharaoh Narmer parades in victory, wearing the red crown of Lower Egypt. Made of siltstone, the palette was most likely used for grinding cosmetics to decorate the statues of the gods in the temple.

I wonder just how many of our modern artefacts will still be around in 5,000 years?

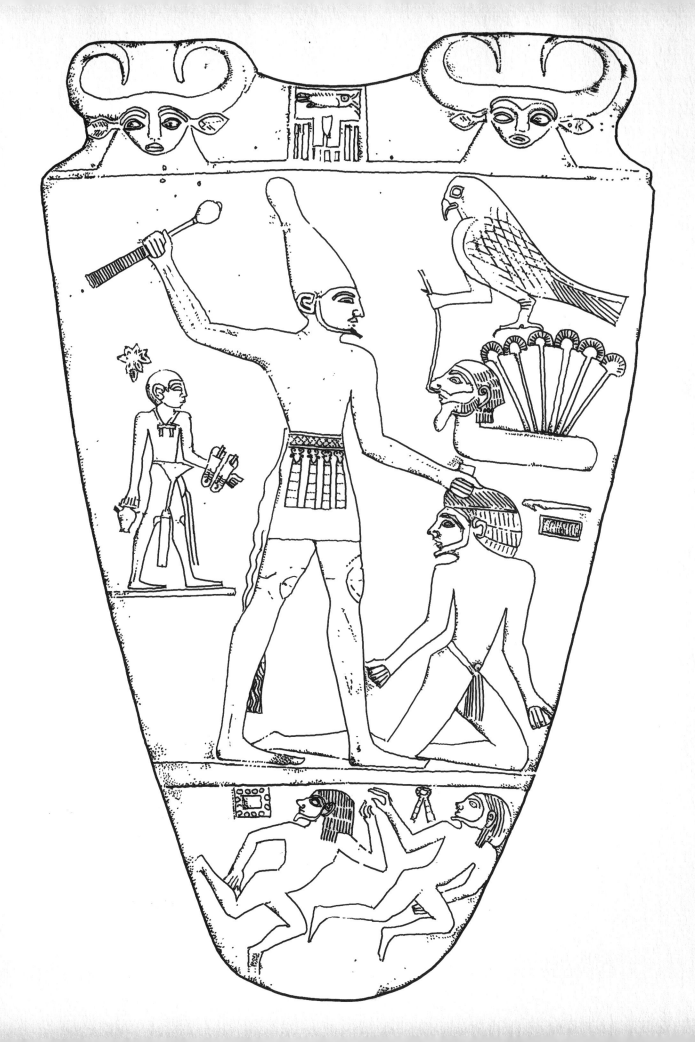

Temple of Horus

Saturday 25th December 1926

The Temple of Horus, built on the supposed site of the mighty battle between Seth and Horus, is the second largest temple in Egypt. It is covered with reliefs that depict a pharaoh smiting his enemies and with images of Horus and Hathor. These reliefs have lost their colour now, but were originally painted in dazzling reds, yellows, blues, greens, and white. Impressive statues of Horus as a hawk stand on each side of the entranceway. These too would have been painted.

Whenever I see a picture or a photograph of the Temple of Horus, I get a strange urge to reach for my brushes and bring it to life once more with a bright, modern palette!

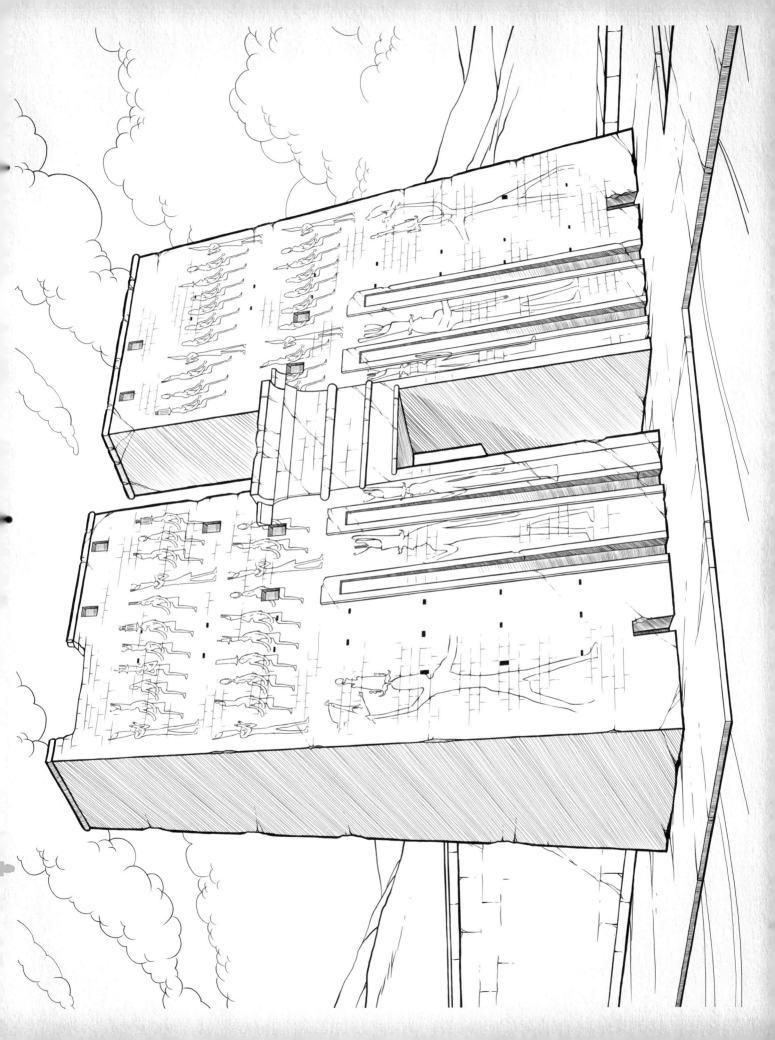

A Trip to Nubia

Friday 31st December 1926

I am anxious to get to Philae, for I now feel sure that is our destination, but I am equally keen to learn as much as I can about Ancient Egypt before starting any excavations. So we are first going south to visit Abu Simbel, in the nearby kingdom of Nubia.

N.H. has drawn Rameses II, styled "the Great" (by Rameses himself) riding in his mighty war chariot. It is interesting to compare this re-creation to the sketch from the wall of Rameses II's granite temple, from which he took inspiration.

Temple of Rameses II

Friday 31st December 1926

Rameses II built this temple to show his dominion over the southern kingdom of Nubia. In 1818, the explorer Belzoni first cleared away enough sand from around its doorway (right) to be able to effect an entry.

Inside, there are two hypostyle halls. The first contains six statues of Osiris. On either side, the walls are covered with reliefs that show Rameses riding his chariot and spearing an enemy. Around 150 feet from the entrance lies the sanctuary—a dark room with four carved seated statues. The temple was built with such accuracy that twice a year at dawn the rays of the sun shine through the doorway and light up these figures.

Back to Philae

Tuesday 4th January 1927

Having enjoyed very much our stay at Abu Simbel, we have turned around and headed back down-river to the granite quarries at Aswan and the Temple of Isis at Philae. In my bones I feel we are closing in on our target, and so I am studying a little more about Ancient Egyptian customs of burial of the dead.

In a ceremony called the Opening of the Mouth, priests prepared the mummy for burial. Priests and mourners read spells to protect the dead man's "ka," or spirit, on its final journey to the other world.

We hired a small sailing boat to take us out to Philae. To our disappointment, we found the ruins were under the water held back by the dam. From Philae, sacred to the goddess Isis, we could see the nearby island of Biga. I could hardly believe my ears when Mr. Taak said that it was once sacred to Osiris, was referred to as the "abaton," or "holy mound," and moreover, that it was relatively unexplored. Why has no one done any more serious excavations? One thing is certain: I will be back for a closer inspection tomorrow!

Mummification

Tuesday 4th January 1927

Ancient Egyptians believed that, in order for the soul to enjoy life after death, the body must be preserved via a process known as mummification. There were many levels of this depending on what one's family could afford. Pharaohs—whose mummies can still be seen to this day— got the most expensive and complete treatment.

FIRST The organs were removed and the brain was hooked out and thrown away. The important organs—intestines, stomach, lungs, and liver—were preserved in canopic jars.

SECOND The corpse was covered in a type of salt called natron and left for a month or so to dry out completely, taking on the appearance of 100-year-old leather.

THIRD Hundreds of yards of linen were wrapped around the corpse. Jewels, charms, and amulets believed to have magical power were added among the bandages.

FOURTH The mummy was wrapped in a sheet and a papyrus scroll of the Book of the Dead—the soul's guide to the afterlife—was placed in the person's hands.

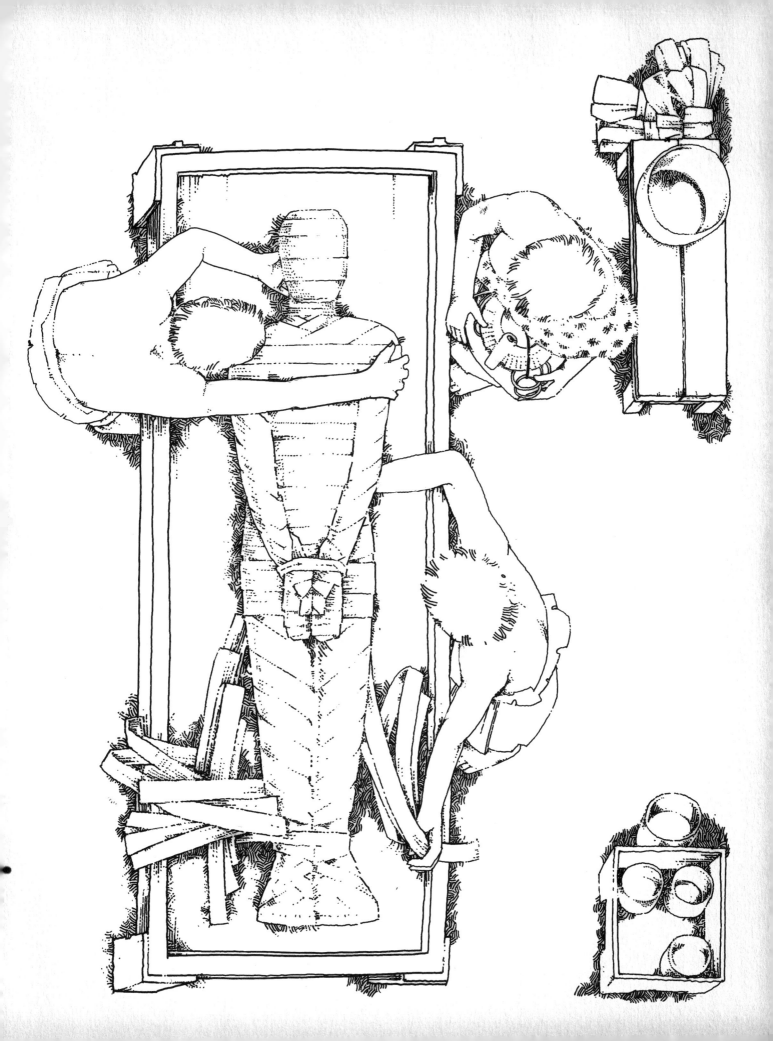

The Book of the Dead

Wednesday 5th January 1927

I can hardly sleep with excitement. Today we went to the island of Biga. I decided I might as well make a few more notes on the Ancient Egyptian idea of the afterlife. After all, if Osiris is the god of the dead, then perhaps in finding his tomb, we should be prepared for almost anything!

MORE ABOUT THE BOOK OF THE DEAD

In Egyptian, this book is called "The Book of Coming Forth By Day." Its spells enable the dead person's "ba," or soul, to take different forms and travel in and out of the tomb. It also includes the judgment of the dead by a panel of gods, in which the dead person's heart is weighed against the feather of truth. The jackal-headed god Anubis weighs the heart, while the ibis-headed Thoth, the god of wisdom, records the verdict. If the dead person is judged "true of voice," then he may pass into the realm of Osiris. If not, his soul is swallowed by the crocodile-headed Ammat, the "devourer."

Thoth

Ammat

Anubis

The Tomb of Osiris?

Wednesday 5th January 1927

In Biga, we found an interesting pit we want to excavate. Beneath the loose earth of the pit, we found a door covered in ancient seal impressions of the name Osiris. In the center is a hollow that seems designed to fit our Eye of Re amulet.

As we were wondering what to do next, a rather strange old lady approached us claiming to be a "priestess of Isis." She warned us about going near the tomb and spoke of dire consequences if we should try to open it, shrieking that the Order of Isis had to keep the tomb of Osiris hidden forever. Her talk of curses has upset me a little, but my companions tell me not to be so silly.

Despite our strange encounter, we have decided, in the interest of science, to try fitting the amulet into the hole tomorrow after we have had a chance to inform the local authorities. Then we will inform the world . . . hopefully of some stupendous finds!!!

> **PUBLISHER'S NOTE:** At this point Emily Sands's journal ends abruptly. Several more pages followed, all of which were blank, save for a few mysterious stains.

PUBLISHER'S NOTE: The aim of Emily's expedition had been to find the lost tomb of Osiris. We may never know if she was correct that the Eye of Re amulet was a "key" that opened the door to a lost tomb in Biga. Unless further clues come to light, the fate of her team—whether they fell afoul of a "mummy's curse," suffered some other dire misadventure, or returned having been sworn to secrecy—may never come to light. However, in the field of Egyptology, exciting new discoveries are made all the time. So who knows?

First U.S. edition 2017

ISBN 978-0-7636-9531-6

17 18 19 20 21 22 WKT 10 9 8 7 6 5 4 3 2 1

Printed in Shenzhen, Guangdong, China

Dugald Steer, Writer
Nick Harris, Artist
Helen Ward, Artist
Douglas Carrel, Artist
Kieran Hood, Senior Designer
Carly Blake, Managing Editor

Candlewick Press
99 Dover Street
Somerville, Massachusetts 02144
www.candlewick.com

www.ologyworld.com